ERIC SLOANE'S
ABCs of
Early Americana

ERIC SLOANE'S
ABCs of
Early Americana

A Sketchbook of Inventions, Curiosities, and Lore

By Eric Sloane

VOYAGEUR PRESS

Cover Design by Maria Friedrich
Printed in China

05   06   07   08   09   5   4   3   2   1

Library of Congress Cataloging-in-Publication Data

Sloane, Eric.
  [ABC book of early Americana]
  Eric Sloane's ABC's of early Americana : a sketchbook of inventions, curiosities, and lore / by Eric Sloane.
    p. cm.
  Originally published as: ABC book of early Americana. Garden City : Doubleday, 1963.
  ISBN 0-89658-687-1 (pbk. : alk. paper)
  1. United States--Social life and customs--Pictorial works. 2. Americana--Pictorial works. 3. Implements, utensils, etc.--United States--Pictorial works. 4. United States--Antiquities--Pictorial works. 5. Americana--Dictionaries. I. Title: ABC's of early Americana. II. Title.
  E161.S52 2005
  973--dc22
                              2005002740

Distributed in Canada by Raincoast Books, 9050 Shaughnessy Street, Vancouver, B.C. V6P 6E5

Published by Voyageur Press, Inc.
123 North Second Street, P.O. Box 338
Stillwater, MN 55082 U.S.A.
651-430-2210, fax 651-430-2211
books@voyageurpress.com
www.voyageurpress.com

Author's note

When I decided to create this A-B-C book, my friends expected to see a *baby's book*. "Of course a few seven-year-olds might glance at it," they said, "but no self-respecting teen-ager would be seen looking at an A-B-C book!"

The fact that I didn't agree is substantiated by this finished book; I think it will both amuse and educate all ages. I don't think that you need be a baby or a mentally retarded person to be fascinated by an alphabet (but grown people just hate to admit that). Businessmen accept their IBM, GE, RKO, CBS, or AT & T; politicians began with their NRA, CCC, WPA, and today almost every official organization is known just by its initials. Even the medical world has branched out from its vitamins, A, B, C, D, E, K, and P into its own world of letters. To be sure, we live in a modern world of FM, TV, FBI, UN, ICBM, A & P, YMCA, and an endless alphabetical category that would baffle great grandfathers.

Yet a century or two ago, people had their own peculiar reverence for the letters of the alphabet. They pondered the alphabet's history and lore; they could become excited about the beauty of the printed page or even one well-formed letter. Actually, the experts of today's advertising art still collect and try to copy the symmetry of early printed pages, yet they will be first to admit these are almost inimitable works of art. Artists used to get delight from drawing their versions of the alphabet; carpenters seldom failed to put their initials and the date on a particularly fine piece of work; children and adults too, made "samplers" of sewed alphabets. Some girls sewed as many as fifty samplers and they certainly were not doing it to learn their A B Cs, for sometimes they were learning Greek and higher mathematics at the same time.

Of course I might be prejudiced, for as a youngster I watched my neighbor, the famed type designer Fred Goudy, as he fashioned his beautiful alphabets. He had gone to the buildings of ancient Greece where he traced letters from the actual stones. Then at home he recreated these letters a yard high, and he often worked a week or a month to get the desired grace and dynamics of only one letter. "My life," he once told me, "is as simple as A B C. But nothing," he added, "is more creative or fascinating."

Later when I left home and became an itinerant sign painter, my stock in trade was primarily a knowledge and a love of the letters of the alphabet.

Nowadays when children have all but lost the ability to write beautifully or clearly, they seem to get no encouragement from their elders who, too, scribble a generally unintelligible hand. In fact, children are now taught, in the very schools that once specialized in fine Spencerian penmanship, to letter their compositions as a defense against illegibility! The banks, however, will not accept a hand-printed name on a check.

This, then, is my argument for the lore and study of the alphabet and its letters: but you will find that this book presents something more. You will find Americana information, I believe, that might throw a new light on some of our early inventions. Most historians say that almost all the early American things were brought over from England or Europe, so with a little research I have tried to collect some of the things that I believe to be *completely ours*. At first I thought there were only a few American things like the rocking chair or the New England salt-box house, but I was delighted to unearth quite a collection of American firsts. I have an idea that the alphabetical arrangement might help us remember these, and I have a suspicion that this book might end up on library tables more than in the nurseries. So happy A B Cs to you! And if you get a bit of the enjoyment that I had in this project, all will have been worth while.

ERIC SLOANE
Weather Hill, Cornwall Bridge, Connecticut

ERIC SLOANE'S
ABCs of
Early Americana

A is for AXE

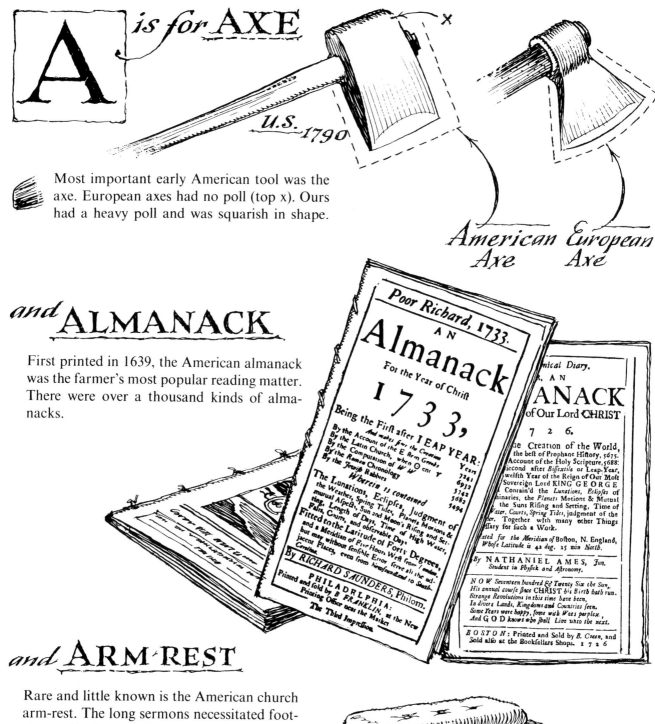

U.S. 1790

American Axe   European Axe

Most important early American tool was the axe. European axes had no poll (top x). Ours had a heavy poll and was squarish in shape.

and ALMANACK

First printed in 1639, the American almanack was the farmer's most popular reading matter. There were over a thousand kinds of almanacks.

and ARM·REST

Rare and little known is the American church arm-rest. The long sermons necessitated footstools, blankets, and arm-rests for comfort.

Shaker arm-rest

about 1790

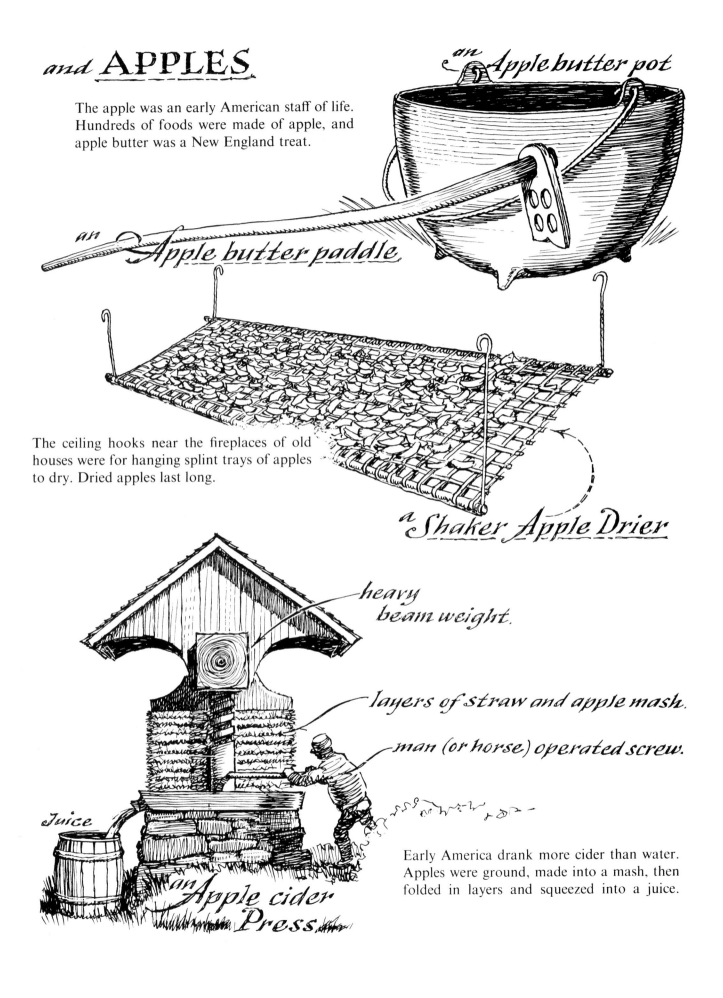

and APPLES

The apple was an early American staff of life. Hundreds of foods were made of apple, and apple butter was a New England treat.

an Apple butter pot

an Apple butter paddle.

The ceiling hooks near the fireplaces of old houses were for hanging splint trays of apples to dry. Dried apples last long.

a Shaker Apple Drier

heavy beam weight.

layers of straw and apple mash.

man (or horse) operated screw.

Juice

an Apple cider Press.

Early America drank more cider than water. Apples were ground, made into a mash, then folded in layers and squeezed into a juice.

B is for BARN

Hitherto big barns were tax banks for the King or the Church, but America had the first large individual barns built by and for the farmers.

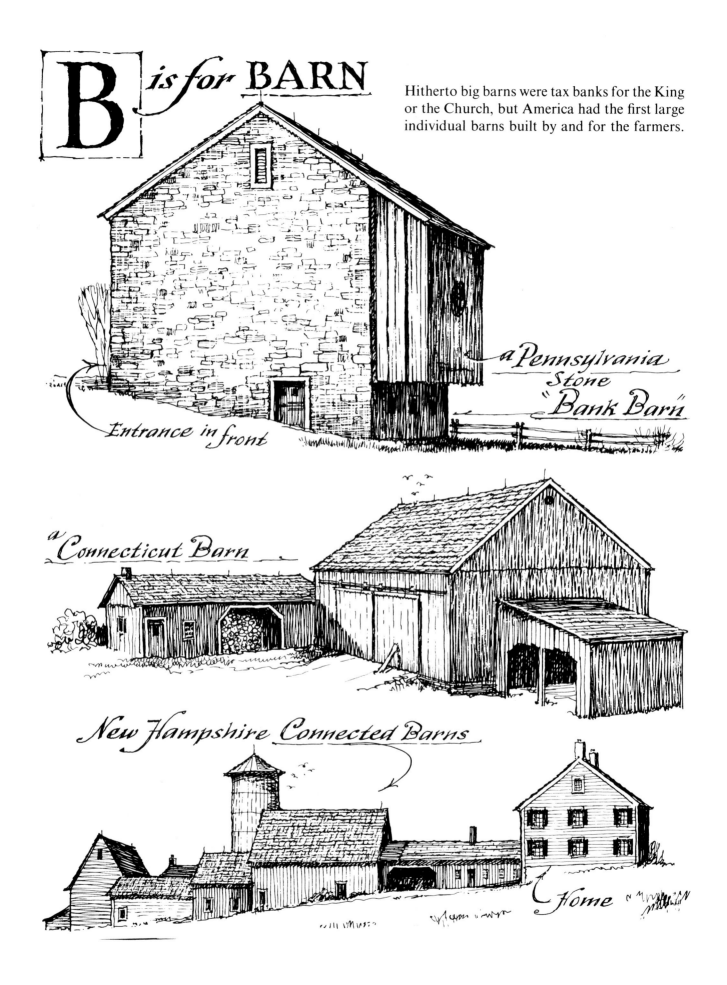

a Pennsylvania Stone "Bank Barn"

Entrance in front

a Connecticut Barn

New Hampshire Connected Barns

Home

and BABY CARRIAGE

Strangely, the first baby carriage was made in America. Charles Burton made it in New York City. Then he went to England to make his "perambulators."

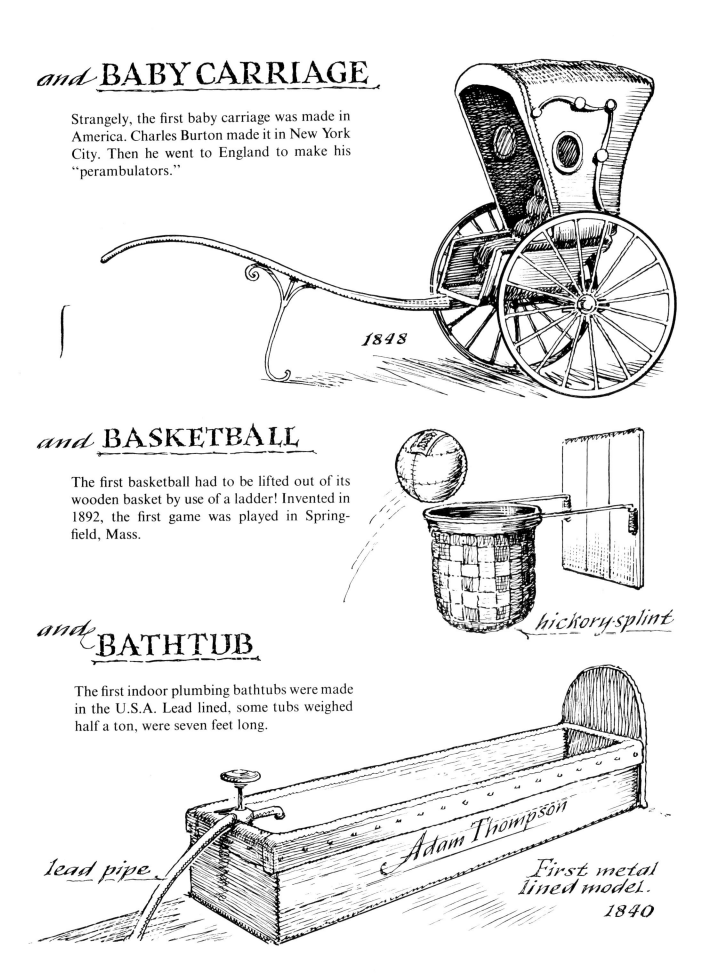

1848

and BASKETBALL

The first basketball had to be lifted out of its wooden basket by use of a ladder! Invented in 1892, the first game was played in Springfield, Mass.

hickory-splint

and BATHTUB

The first indoor plumbing bathtubs were made in the U.S.A. Lead lined, some tubs weighed half a ton, were seven feet long.

lead pipe

Adam Thompson

First metal lined model.

1840

C is for COVERED BRIDGE

Copying the Philadelphia "Permanent Bridge" of 1805, all American bridges added roofs and began our covered-bridge architecture.

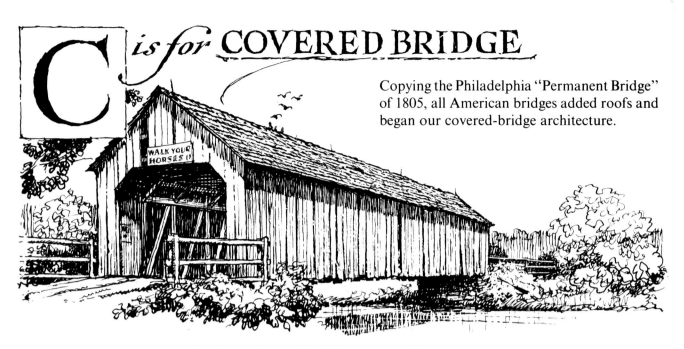

and CONESTOGA WAGON

The Conestoga wagon of 1760 was "the world's finest wagon." It had wide tires, a tentlike living space, and a boatlike wagon-body.

and CIGAR-STORE INDIAN

The wooden cigar-store Indian of yesterday is already accepted as rare Americana art.

and COAL

Hard coal was discovered in Pennsylvania in 1791 but it was not thought burnable. "Coals" were once wood embers to start fires with.

a "Coal" Pan

and CHOP SUEY

Chop suey is not Chinese but Americana, being invented in 1896 in New York City.

and CORNHUSK DOLL

The first early American dolls were made of cornhusks, tied with vines, dyed with berry juices. They were copies of Indian dolls.

1780

and COFFEE

At the time of the Boston Tea Party, America used as much tea as the English. But coffee then took tea's place and became "American."

Coffee roaster 1760

George Washington's Coffee Grinder

and CANDY

Only one hundred years ago, candy was a verb meaning "to preserve with sugar." When you ate "candy" it was raw sugar scissored from a loaf.

Sugar Cutters produced "Candy."

D is for DOG·MILL

Dogs were used for churning butter, turning fireplace spits, and many other early chores.

Churn

and DUGOUT

The dugout canoe is American. When the first pioneers arrived, they marveled at the big one-piece wooden "canoes" of the red Indians.

and DUTCH OVEN

The Dutch oven is either an iron pot with lid for coals or a reflector "tin kitchen." Iron-door wall ovens are not Dutch ovens.

Hot coals on the lid

1720

"tin kitchen" reflector oven

1800

and DEVIL'S FIDDLE

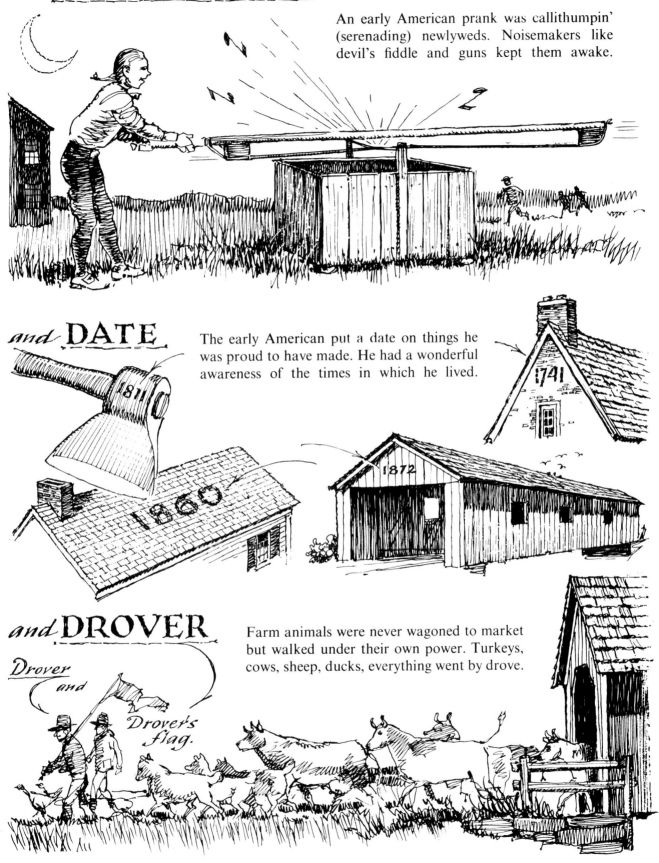

An early American prank was callithumpin' (serenading) newlyweds. Noisemakers like devil's fiddle and guns kept them awake.

and DATE

The early American put a date on things he was proud to have made. He had a wonderful awareness of the times in which he lived.

and DROVER

Farm animals were never wagoned to market but walked under their own power. Turkeys, cows, sheep, ducks, everything went by drove.

Drover and

Drover's flag.

E is for EAR TRUMPET

The only hearing aid two centuries ago was the ear trumpet. Made of tin, there were a great many strange ones like the one shown.

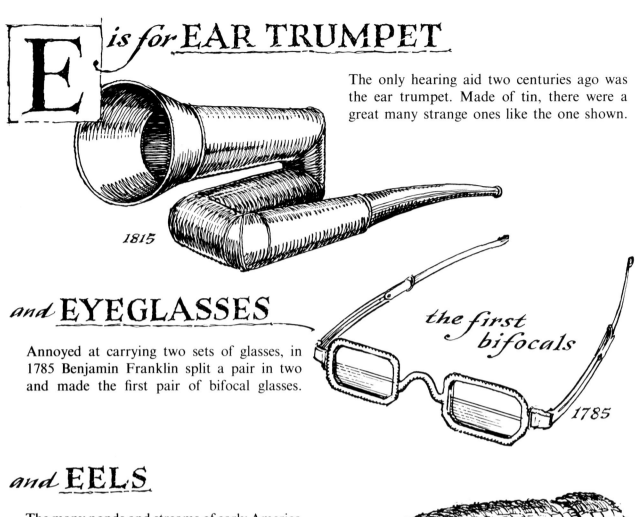

1815

and EYEGLASSES

Annoyed at carrying two sets of glasses, in 1785 Benjamin Franklin split a pair in two and made the first pair of bifocal glasses.

the first bifocals

1785

and EELS

The many ponds and streams of early America bred vast numbers of eels. In old-time barns you will still find eel traps and eel forks.

Hickory Eel trap

Eel forks

and ENVELOPE

Letters were just folded over and sealed. The first manufacturer of envelopes was a Mr. Pearson who began making them in 1839 in New York.

To Benjamin Franklin Esq
141 Market St
Philadelphia
Penna

All Mail was on one sheet

and ELL·RULE

An early American measuring device was the ell-rule. Now completely forgotten, the ell was a yard and one quarter, used mostly for cloth.

45 inches

and EARMARK

Livestock were once earmarked (as they are now branded). Cattle were allowed to wander, but earmarks were recorded at the town hall.

and ELECTION TORCH

The election torch was a lard-oil lamp that started as a farm lantern. Just a tin can that hung on a swivel, it burned in wind or rain.

and "ENTERTAINMENT"

Early American inn signs used the word "entertainment" in its true meaning, the serving of food and lodging. Just that.

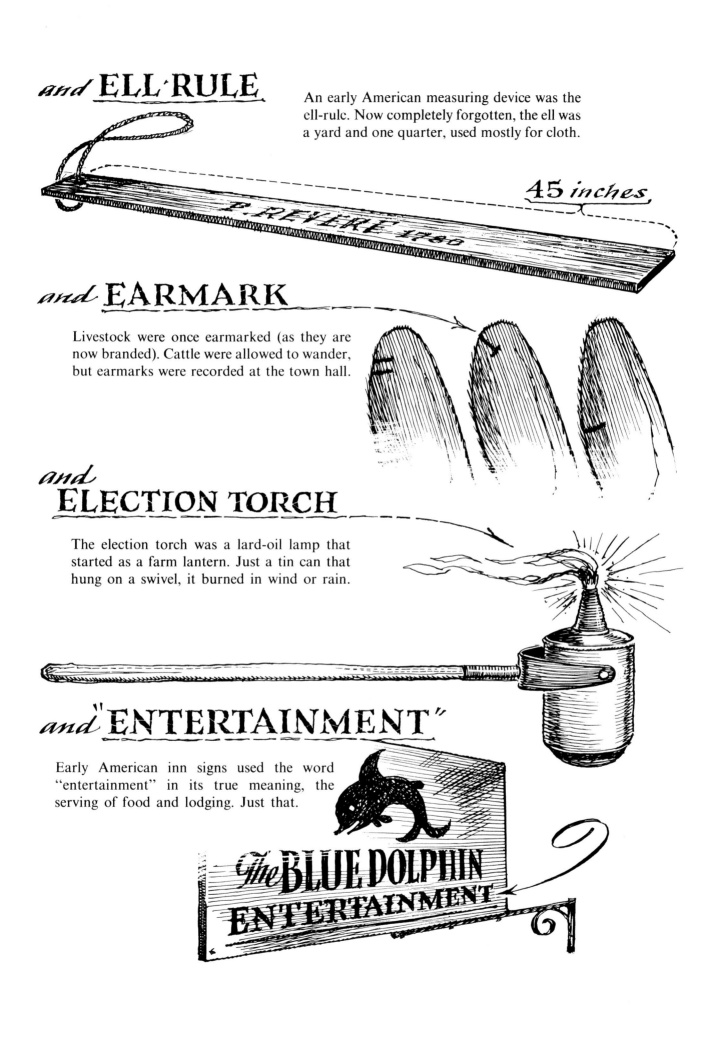

The BLUE DOLPHIN ENTERTAINMENT

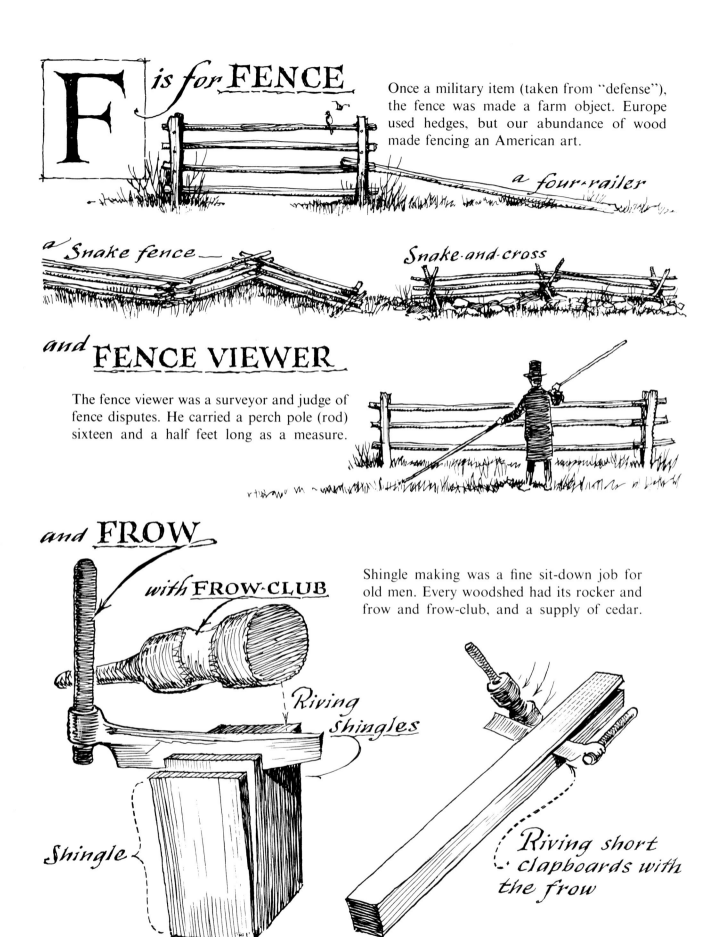

F is for FENCE

Once a military item (taken from "defense"), the fence was made a farm object. Europe used hedges, but our abundance of wood made fencing an American art.

a four-railer

a snake fence

Snake-and-cross

and FENCE VIEWER

The fence viewer was a surveyor and judge of fence disputes. He carried a perch pole (rod) sixteen and a half feet long as a measure.

and FROW

with FROW-CLUB

Riving Shingles

Shingle

Shingle making was a fine sit-down job for old men. Every woodshed had its rocker and frow and frow-club, and a supply of cedar.

Riving short clapboards with the frow

and FOOT STOVES

Foot stoves were used in church, under the blankets in sleighs and stagecoaches. The heat came from charcoal contained in a pan.

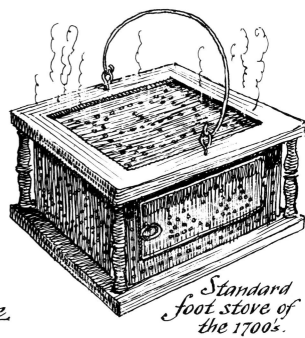

Standard foot stove of the 1700's.

Sleigh stove

and FIRE·BACK

Before the time of firebrick, the rear of fireplaces was often covered with sheets of iron which reflected additional warmth.

and FRAME·SAW

Saws were once stretched between two arms in a frame. They were also called bow saws. The blade could be turned on turn-handles.

arm

turn-handle

toggle

G is for GIANT HOGSHEAD

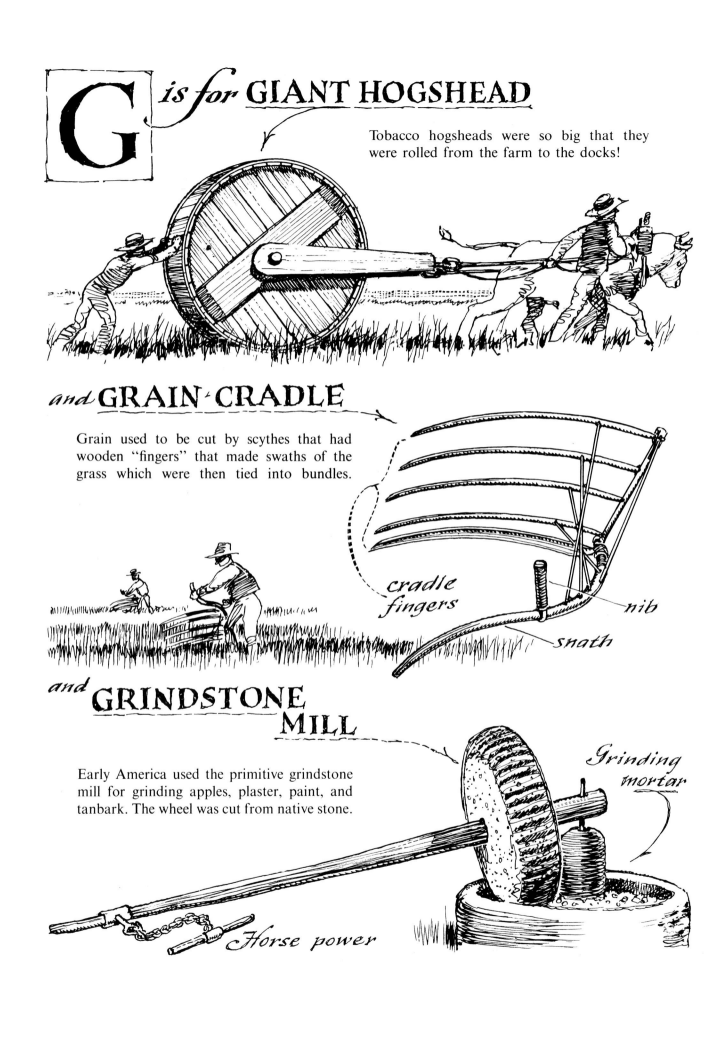

Tobacco hogsheads were so big that they were rolled from the farm to the docks!

and GRAIN·CRADLE

Grain used to be cut by scythes that had wooden "fingers" that made swaths of the grass which were then tied into bundles.

cradle fingers

nib

snath

and GRINDSTONE MILL

Early America used the primitive grindstone mill for grinding apples, plaster, paint, and tanbark. The wheel was cut from native stone.

Grinding mortar

Horse power

and GOOSEWING·AXE

Rarest of the broadaxes are the goose-wing types. They were made before the eighteen hundreds, copied from old German patterns.

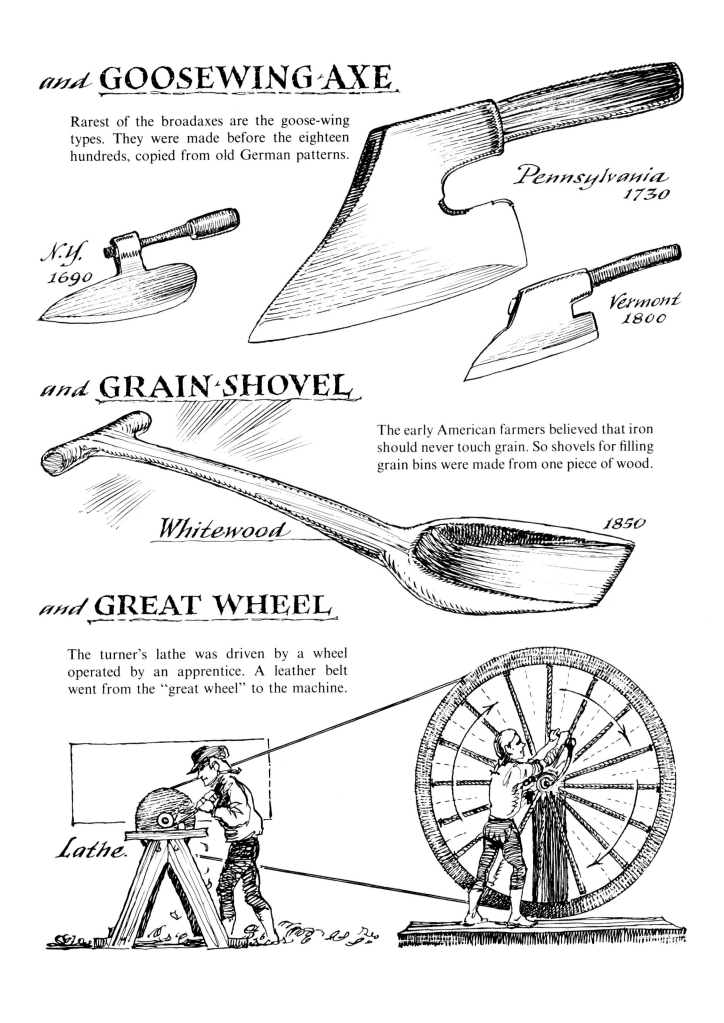

Pennsylvania
1730

N.Y.
1690

Vermont
1800

and GRAIN·SHOVEL

The early American farmers believed that iron should never touch grain. So shovels for filling grain bins were made from one piece of wood.

Whitewood

1850

and GREAT WHEEL

The turner's lathe was driven by a wheel operated by an apprentice. A leather belt went from the "great wheel" to the machine.

Lathe.

H *is for* HORSEPOWER

Horsepower ran sawmills, tanbark mills, paint mills, gristmills, threshing mills, even machinery for operating ferryboats!

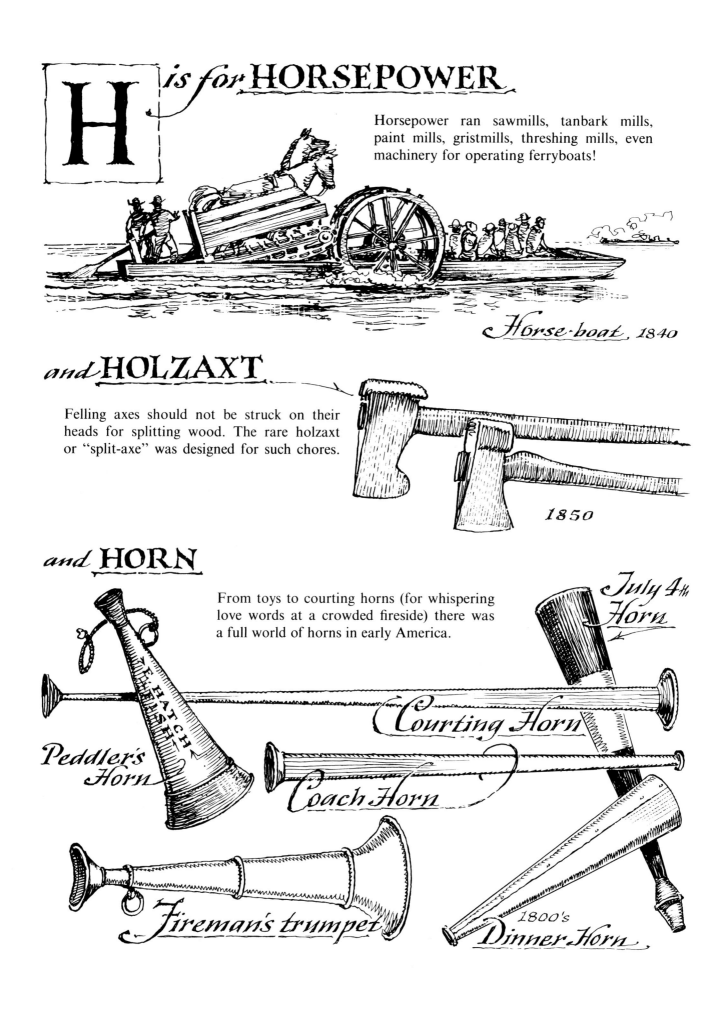

Horse-boat, 1840

and HOLZAXT

Felling axes should not be struck on their heads for splitting wood. The rare holzaxt or "split-axe" was designed for such chores.

1850

and HORN

From toys to courting horns (for whispering love words at a crowded fireside) there was a full world of horns in early America.

July 4th Horn

Courting Horn

Peddler's Horn

Coach Horn

Fireman's trumpet

1800's Dinner Horn

and HARROW

As soon as the ground was clear of stones, the harrow was used for scratching and for leveling. The first harrows were all wood.

oak spikes

and HEX·SIGNS

No more weird than our "lucky horseshoe," the Pennsylvania barn ornament was no more than a design (except to a few superstitious farmers).

and HAY FORK

Early American hay forks were made of one piece of wood. Here are three types, two of split prongs and wedges, one natural.

wedges

three prong

Six prong

Natural fork

I is for ICE CREAM

1784

Ice cream is early American! It was sold by Mr. Hall in New York City in 1785, but George Washington in 1784 bought a newly invented "ice cream machine."

and ICE·BOAT

When the roads were closed by winter, the ice-boat was used on the Hudson River first as a sled. In 1790 Oliver Booth added a mast and sail.

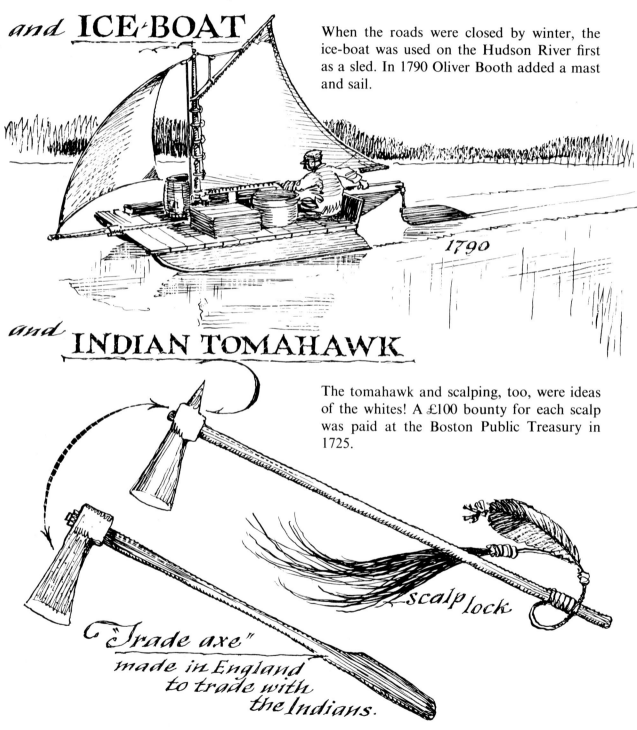

1790

and INDIAN TOMAHAWK

The tomahawk and scalping, too, were ideas of the whites! A £100 bounty for each scalp was paid at the Boston Public Treasury in 1725.

scalp lock

"Trade axe" made in England to trade with the Indians.

and INKWELL

Fountain pens and ball-points make the ink-well antique. The early "inkpot" had a sand shaker for drying the ink (before blotters).

Stoneware 1810

Glass 1850

for sprinkling sand

Ink dryer

and IRONS

From the early word for "heavy," a "sad" iron was solid, while the others were hollow, with compartment for hot coals or burning charcoal.

"Tailor's Goose"

Hollow Charcoal-iron

Sad iron

Corncob handle

and ICE

In 1799 the first commercial ice was cut and shipped from Canal Street, New York City, and sent to South Carolina. Ice was a major United States business.

J is for JACK·O'·LANTERN

Early American word "Jack-a-Lent" meant a silly fellow. Both pumpkin (from the archaic word, pompion) and jack-o'-lantern are of New England derivation.

and JOHNNY·CAKE

The word "johnny-cake" was first "journey-cake," for it was a cake made during a journey and baked against a flat board before the fire.

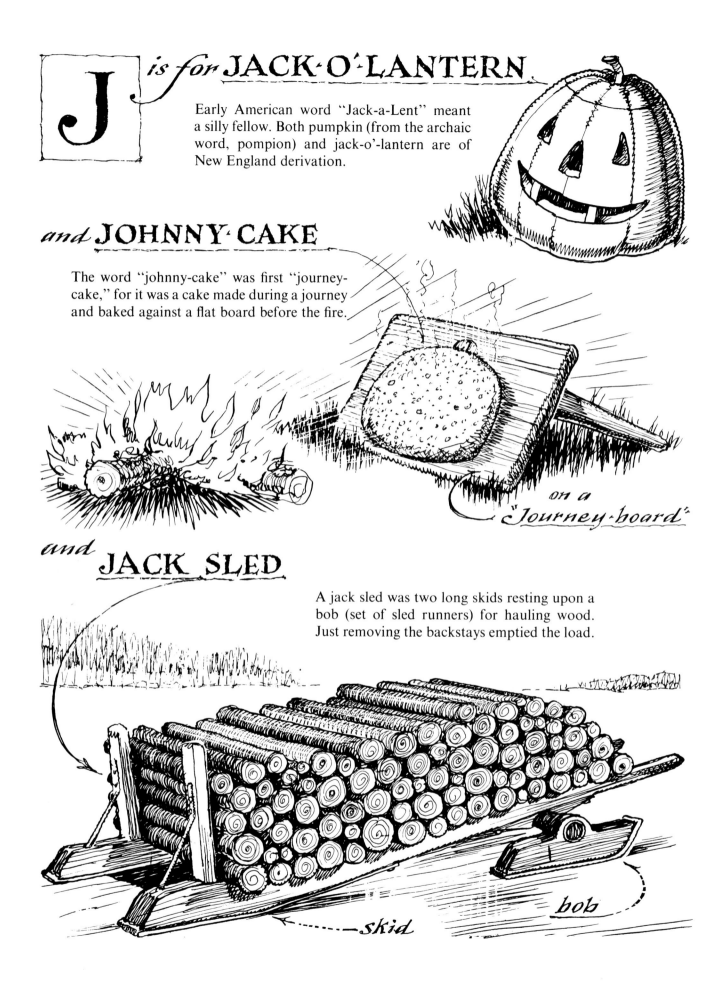

on a "Journey·board"

and JACK SLED

A jack sled was two long skids resting upon a bob (set of sled runners) for hauling wood. Just removing the backstays emptied the load.

skid

bob

and JUMP SCOOTER

An almost forgotten early American toy, the jump scooter was merely a seat on a barrel stave but it took more skill than sledding.

and JINGLE BELLS

Jingle bell was the old-time name for crotal bell, the small cylinder bell. They were made in Easthampton, Connecticut, "Jingletown, U.S.A."

and JOUNCING SEAT

Appearing even before the rocking chair, the jouncing seat (also called wagon-spring seat) proved too clumsy for small farmhouse rooms.

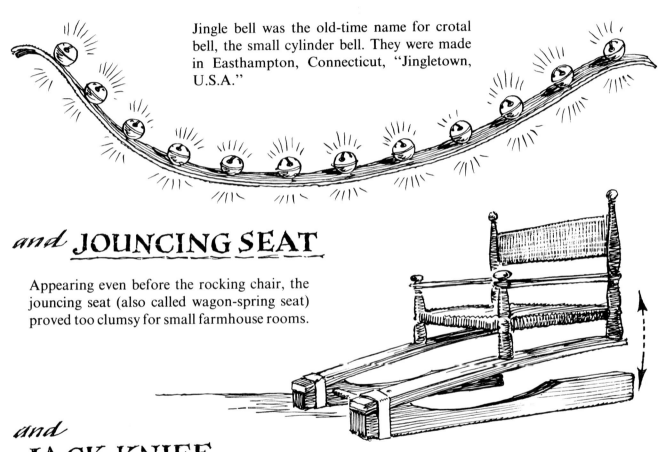

and JACKKNIFE

Called the jack-spring knife in the 1800's, the name was shortened later in the 1800's to jackknife.

Yankee Jack
1860

K is for KINGPOST TRUSS

The first American bridges were wooden kingpost trusses. Note how weight will make each piece push against the other.

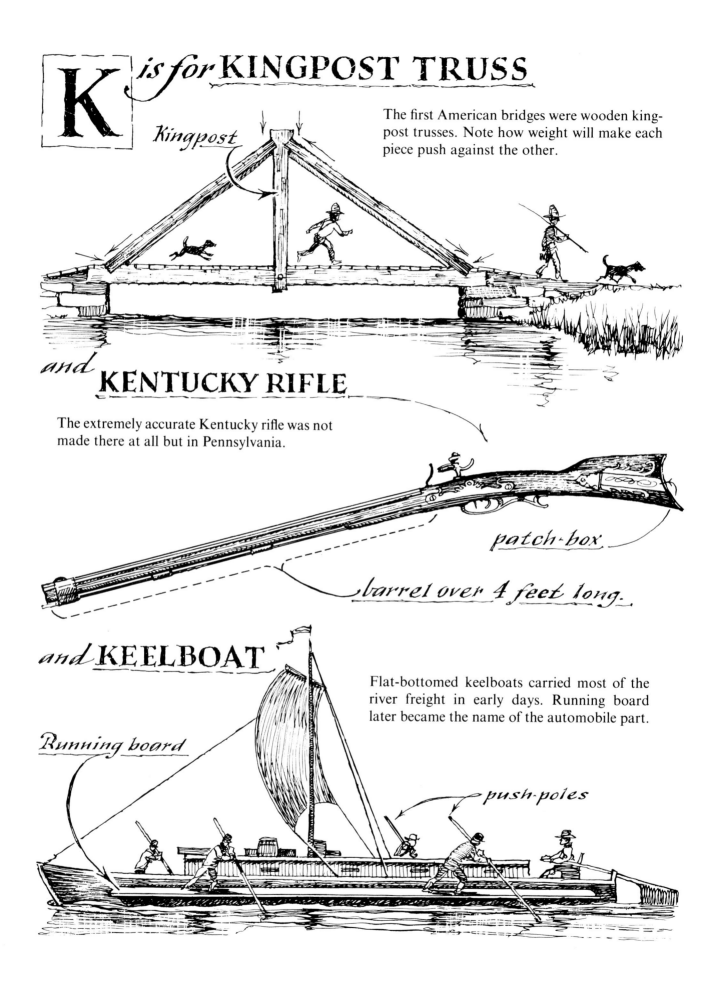

Kingpost

and KENTUCKY RIFLE

The extremely accurate Kentucky rifle was not made there at all but in Pennsylvania.

patch-box

barrel over 4 feet long.

and KEELBOAT

Flat-bottomed keelboats carried most of the river freight in early days. Running board later became the name of the automobile part.

Running board

push-poles

and KITCHEN *Utensils*

Kitchenware was often made of fruit woods. Bowls and dippers were made of burl woods which are the lumpy masses seen on trees.

Grater

tin

Dipper

Burl wood

Chopper

Sap Pail

Strainer with arms to rest on dish.

Pastry Stamp

Ladle of apple burl.

Butter Spoon

whitewood

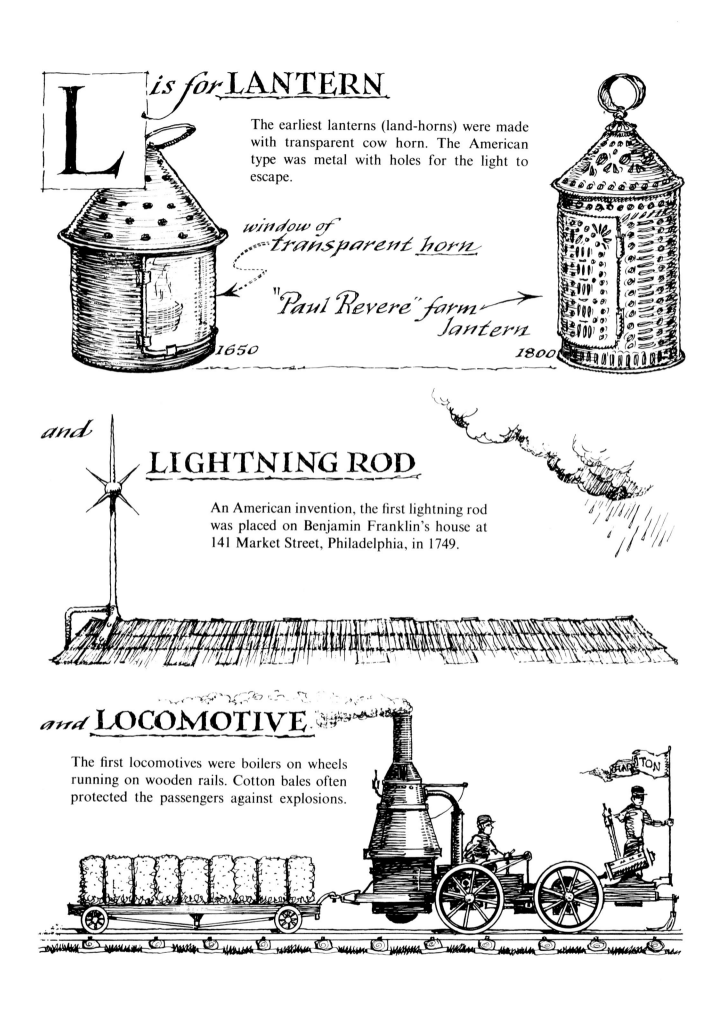

L is for LANTERN

The earliest lanterns (land-horns) were made with transparent cow horn. The American type was metal with holes for the light to escape.

window of transparent horn

"Paul Revere" farm lantern

1650

1800

and

LIGHTNING ROD

An American invention, the first lightning rod was placed on Benjamin Franklin's house at 141 Market Street, Philadelphia, in 1749.

and LOCOMOTIVE

The first locomotives were boilers on wheels running on wooden rails. Cotton bales often protected the passengers against explosions.

and LOG CABIN

The first American houses were split wood and mud. Log cabins came later. Here shown below are typical early log cabin notches.

bark roof

Saddle notch 1800

Sharp notch

Square notch

and LEAD PENCIL

The early pencils were sawed strips of lead cased between two wood covers, unlike today's round graphite rods in their wooden coverings.

lead

wood cases

and LEVEL

When America was young, floors and doors did not have to be so level; there were no spirit levels. Just a weight and right angle sufficed.

A plumb-bob Builder's Level.

lead weight

M is for MINT

In early American times, mint was a major farming crop, used for tea and medicines. Crushed mint with hot water made the tea.

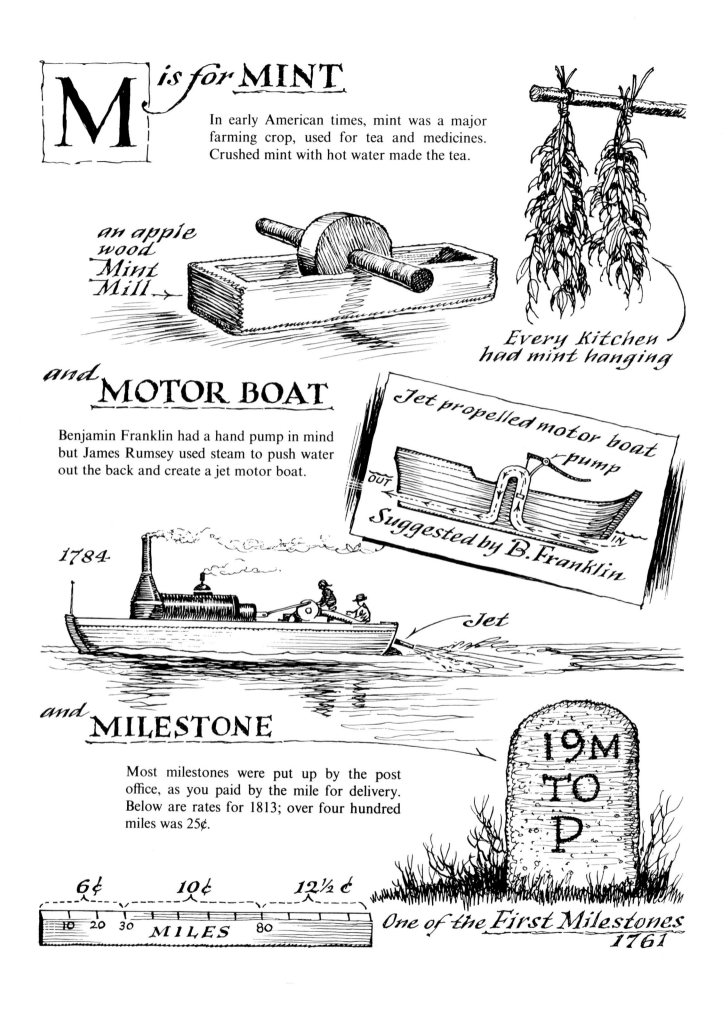

an apple wood Mint Mill →

Every Kitchen had mint hanging

and MOTOR BOAT

Benjamin Franklin had a hand pump in mind but James Rumsey used steam to push water out the back and create a jet motor boat.

Jet propelled motor boat pump

OUT IN

Suggested by B. Franklin

1784

Jet

and MILESTONE

Most milestones were put up by the post office, as you paid by the mile for delivery. Below are rates for 1813; over four hundred miles was 25¢.

19M TO P

6¢   10¢   12½¢

10 20 30   MILES   80

One of the First Milestones
1761

and MORTICE CHISEL

As cheap nails and mass production arrived, craftsmanship waned. Pieces were once held together by mortice and tenon, the best way.

tenon

mortice

pin

and MUD·HORSE

True there used to be more mud in the old days, but this rig was for clam digging in Europe long before we used it on the farm.

and MUFF

An American invention, the muff was first used by men, often to carry inks or other materials to work on extremely cold days.

Bearskin muff of the 1700's

and MINER'S CANDLE

A miner's candle could be hung on a nail or hammered into rock, but the pioneers of early America made wall lights out of them.

N is for NUTMEG

In early times people carried nutmegs with them to flavor food or drinks. Tin graters were for men, silver for the ladies.

Kitchen Grater

Pocket Graters

Sliding Grater

and NOON MARK

All early houses had "noon marks" cut into window sills or doorways to mark the time of day. They were mostly for summer chores.

and NAILS

The earliest nails were hand wrought: they tapered on all four sides. Cut nails (after 1800) were flat, tapering only on one side.

WROUGHT NAIL

CUT NAIL

tapered on all sides

tapered on top

not tapered on side

a Nail Header for wrought nails

and NEW ENGLAND

Other than a boiled dinner, Yankee peddler, maple-sugar sap house, stone fences, or rare coins, few things are known as "New England."

New England Shilling
MASSACHUSETTS, 1652

New England Sap house

New England Stone fence

New England Peddler

New England Boiled Dinner

and NIDDY NODDY

"Niddy noddy, two heads on one body!" went an old American ditty. This strange thing is a reel. It winds and then measures yarn.

18 in.

wound

unwound

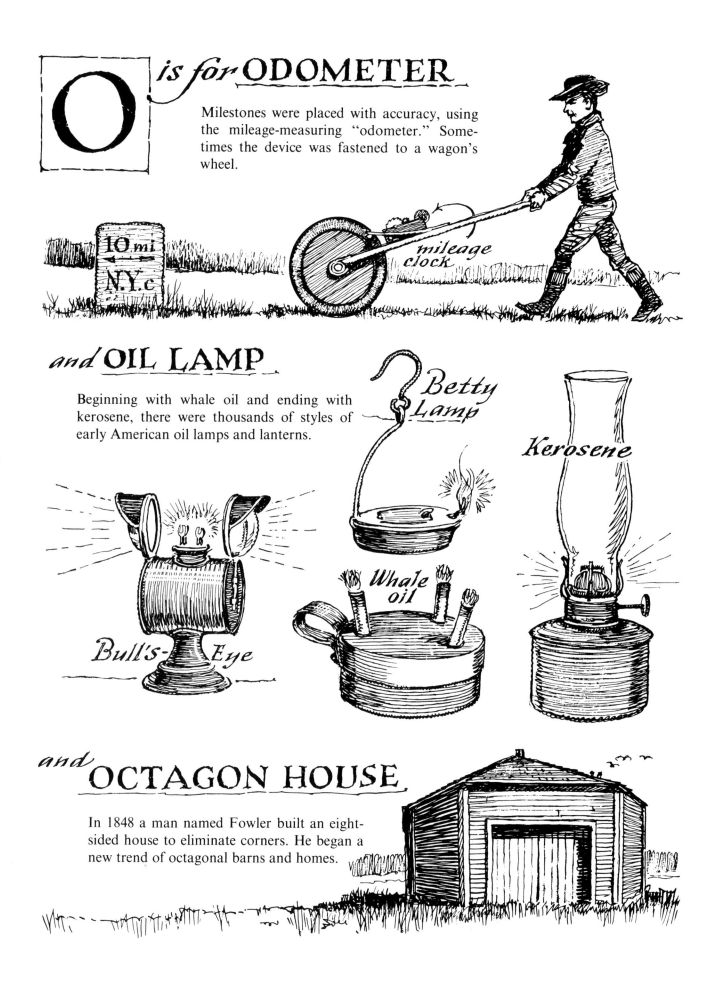

O is for ODOMETER

Milestones were placed with accuracy, using the mileage-measuring "odometer." Sometimes the device was fastened to a wagon's wheel.

mileage clock

10 mi ← N.Y.c

and OIL LAMP

Beginning with whale oil and ending with kerosene, there were thousands of styles of early American oil lamps and lanterns.

Betty Lamp

Kerosene

Bull's-Eye

Whale oil

and OCTAGON HOUSE

In 1848 a man named Fowler built an eight-sided house to eliminate corners. He began a new trend of octagonal barns and homes.

and OUTHOUSES

Though the privy has now claimed the name, "outhouse" was once the name for any added outbuilding on the early American farmland.

The early privy had a Crescent ("LUNAR" IS FEMININE) and a Sun (MASCULINE) to designate MEN and WOMEN.

and more Outhouses...

an Overhang Wash House

a Well House

a Spring House

a Butchering House

a Farm Forge Barn

P *is for* PADDLE·BOAT

An American first, the first steamboat to carry a man was built by John Fitch, 1786. Before the paddle wheel, it used 12 paddles.

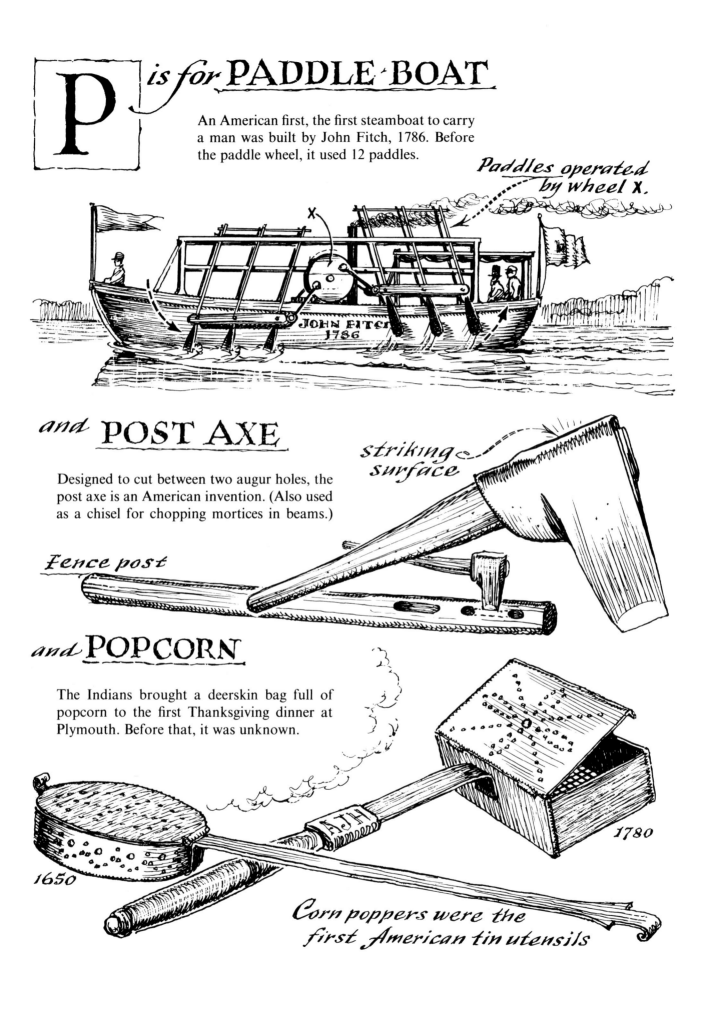

Paddles operated by wheel X.

JOHN FITCH 1786

and POST AXE

Designed to cut between two augur holes, the post axe is an American invention. (Also used as a chisel for chopping mortices in beams.)

striking surface

fence post

and POPCORN

The Indians brought a deerskin bag full of popcorn to the first Thanksgiving dinner at Plymouth. Before that, it was unknown.

1650

1780

Corn poppers were the first American tin utensils

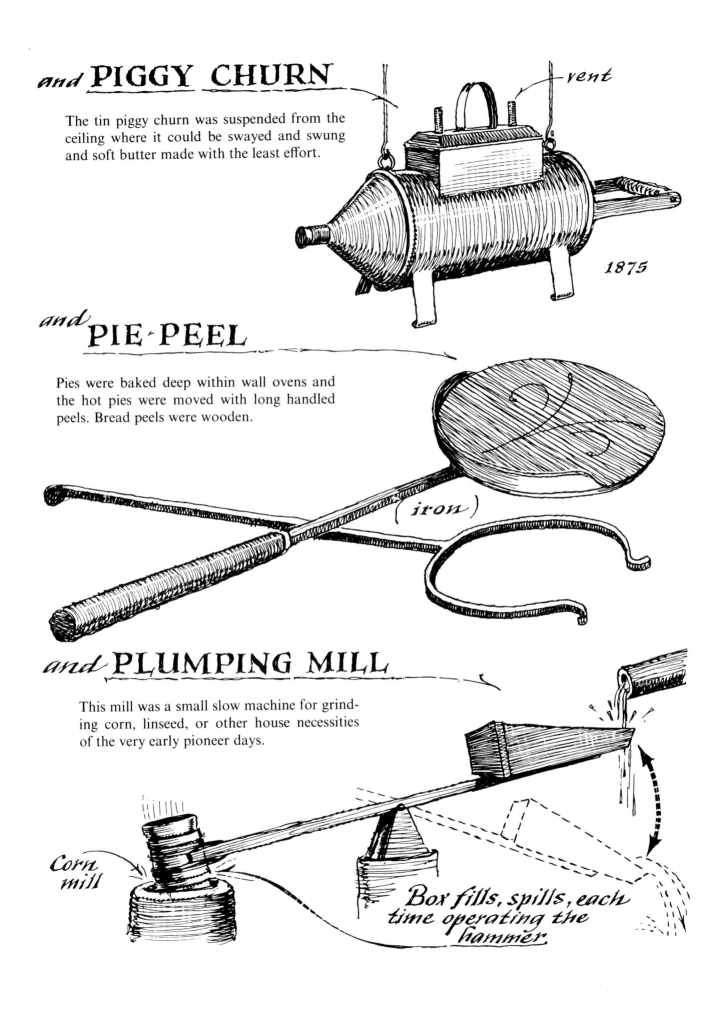

and PIGGY CHURN

The tin piggy churn was suspended from the ceiling where it could be swayed and swung and soft butter made with the least effort.

vent

1875

and PIE-PEEL

Pies were baked deep within wall ovens and the hot pies were moved with long handled peels. Bread peels were wooden.

(*iron*)

and PLUMPING MILL

This mill was a small slow machine for grinding corn, linseed, or other house necessities of the very early pioneer days.

Corn mill

Box fills, spills, each time operating the hammer

Q is for QUEENPOST truss

Two upright posts with a cross between is the queenpost bridge truss. Nearly all the small covered bridges were queenpost type.

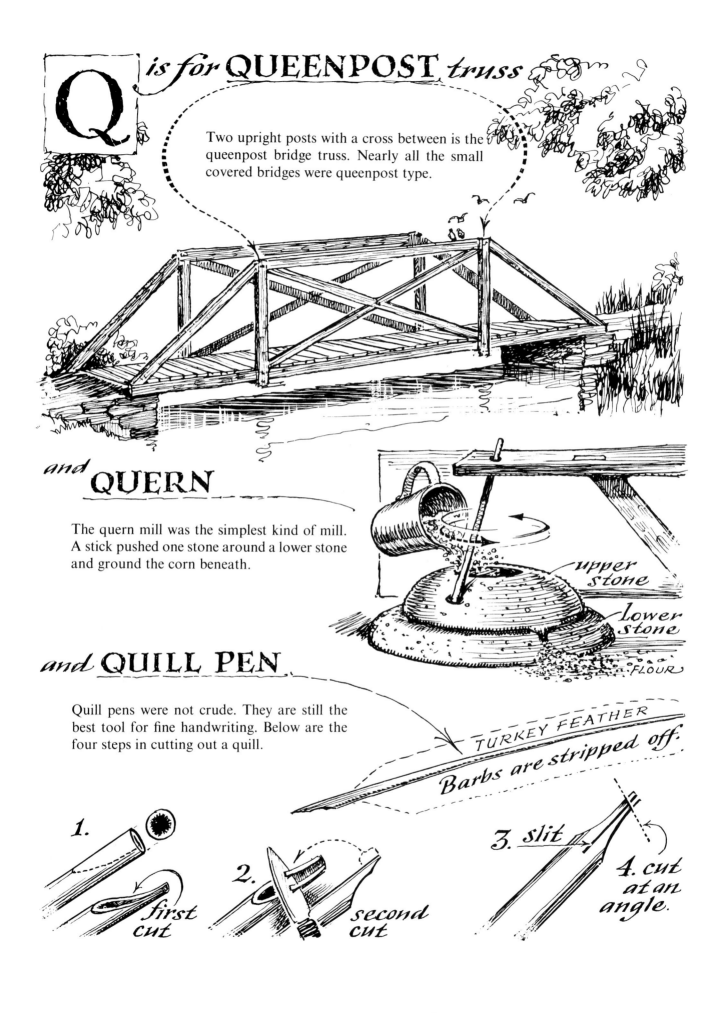

and QUERN

The quern mill was the simplest kind of mill. A stick pushed one stone around a lower stone and ground the corn beneath.

upper stone

lower stone

FLOUR

and QUILL PEN

Quill pens were not crude. They are still the best tool for fine handwriting. Below are the four steps in cutting out a quill.

TURKEY FEATHER

Barbs are stripped off.

1. *first cut*

2. *second cut*

3. *slit*

4. *cut at an angle.*

Q is QUARRY SLED

People wonder how the old-timers moved the gigantic stones for building. They sledded them in winter, rolled the sled in summer!

and QUICK·HEDGE

The word "quick" at one time meant "alive." Hence: quick-hedge (live hedge), quick-stock (livestock), quick-wine (live wine), "quick and the dead," etc.

and QUAKER

Quakers were supposed to "quake in the sight of the Lord," just as Shakers shook. But Quakers now call themselves Friends (and quake no more).

Old Quaker costume and Meeting House

and QUOINSTONES

Wall builders always locked corners with big quoinstones which were massive, flat, and long corner rocks that overlapped at right angles.

Shown by dark stones.

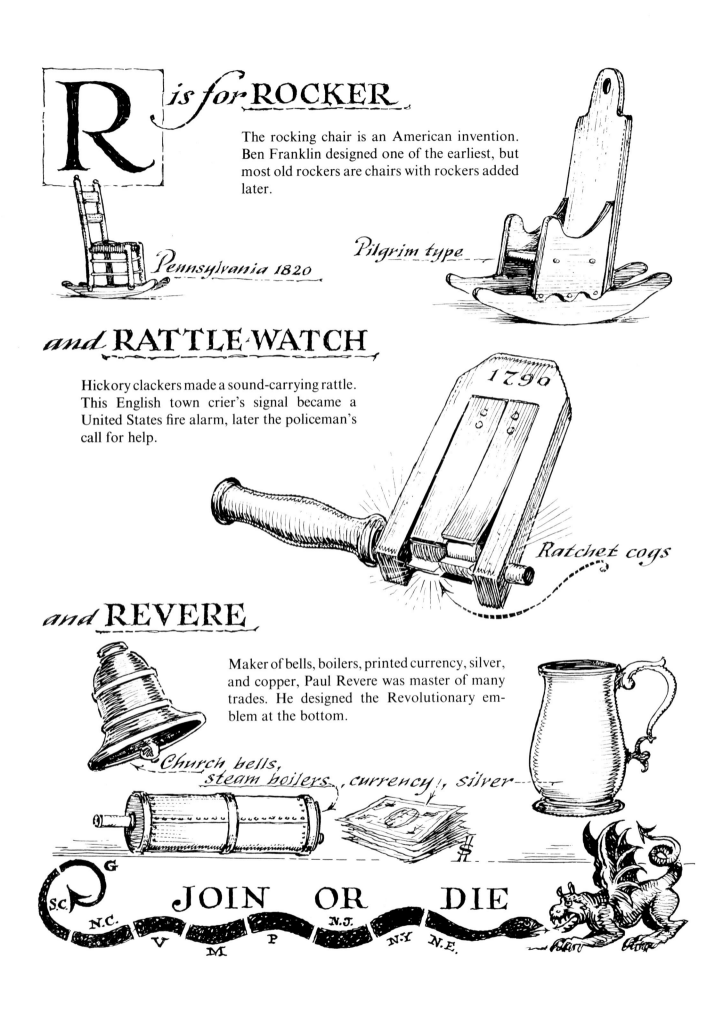

R is for ROCKER

The rocking chair is an American invention. Ben Franklin designed one of the earliest, but most old rockers are chairs with rockers added later.

Pennsylvania 1820

Pilgrim type

and RATTLE·WATCH

Hickory clackers made a sound-carrying rattle. This English town crier's signal became a United States fire alarm, later the policeman's call for help.

1790

Ratchet cogs

and REVERE

Maker of bells, boilers, printed currency, silver, and copper, Paul Revere was master of many trades. He designed the Revolutionary emblem at the bottom.

Church bells, steam boilers, currency, silver

JOIN OR DIE

S.C. G N.C. V M P N.J. N.Y. N.E.

and RUSH LIGHT

The rush wick held in an iron rush clamp was replaced by the candle which gave more light, less smoke, and lasted much longer.

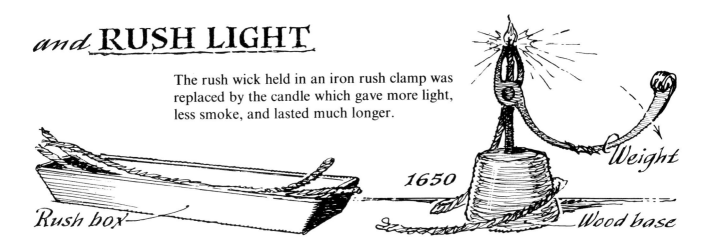

1650

Weight

Rush box

Wood base

and "RUBBERS"

known once as Rubber Shoes, or Gum Shoes

The first rubber shoes were made in America in 1820 but they melted in good weather and smelled bad. They were perfected in 1842.

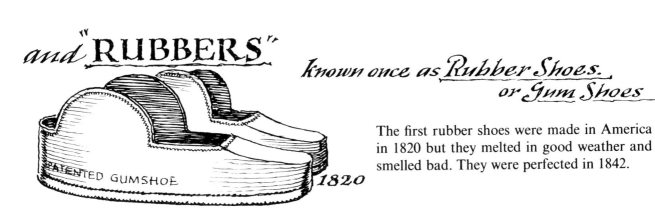

PATENTED GUMSHOE

1820

and RAIL SPLITTING

Once a profession (Lincoln worked at it) this was done with gluts (wooden wedges) struck by a huge hammer (beetle) to make fence railing.

Beetle and Gluts

S is for SALTBOX

At first added to a house as a lean-to (X) the New England saltbox became a standard American house design as early as the middle 1700's.

SALT

and SNOW·ROLLER

The smoothest roads used to be snow-packed ones of winter. People worked very hard to keep the roads snow filled and packed down tight with rollers.

rock weight

and STONE·BOAT

Stone-boats were flat toboggans used to slide huge boulders and heavy burdens over grass or muddy fields. Some people even went to town on them.

and SLEDS

For every wagon, the early farmer had about six sleds, for all heavy loads were moved in winter. Each chore had its own type of sled.

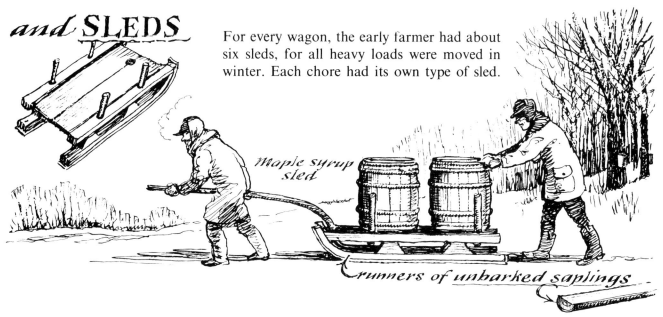

Maple syrup sled

runners of unbarked saplings

and STOVES

First fed from outside, then in a fireplace, then a "fire in an iron box," kitchen stoves were created in America by Pennsylvanians.

outside the house

Inside

①

Kitchen

bed room

②

a Shaker stove

③

and SLEIGHS

American sleighs were works of art. Their fragile grace was as efficient as it was a delight to the eye. Many were used as racers.

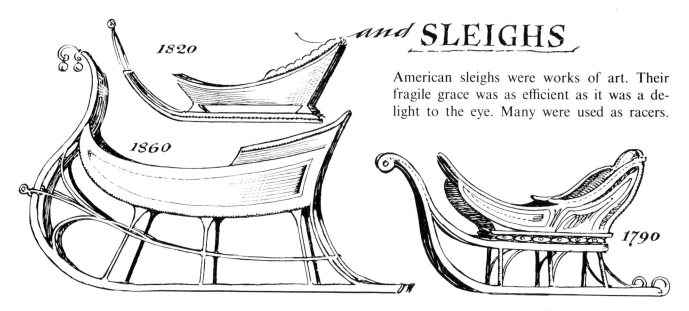

1820

1860

1790

T is for TEPEE

A completely American word, "tepee" is taken from the Siouan language, "ti" meaning "dwell" and "pi" meaning "used for" (used for dwelling).

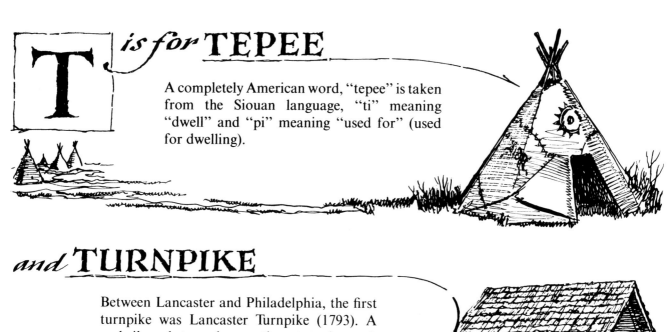

and TURNPIKE

Between Lancaster and Philadelphia, the first turnpike was Lancaster Turnpike (1793). A real pike pole turned across the gate to the road.

PAY TOLL

Pike

and TORNADO

The first and second tornadoes which were recorded were in New Haven, 1682 and 1839.

and TRACTORS

Dr. Elisha Perkins' "Metallic Tractors" were two pointed bars that were supposed to cure body pain when drawn across the sore spot.

Brass

Steel

1790

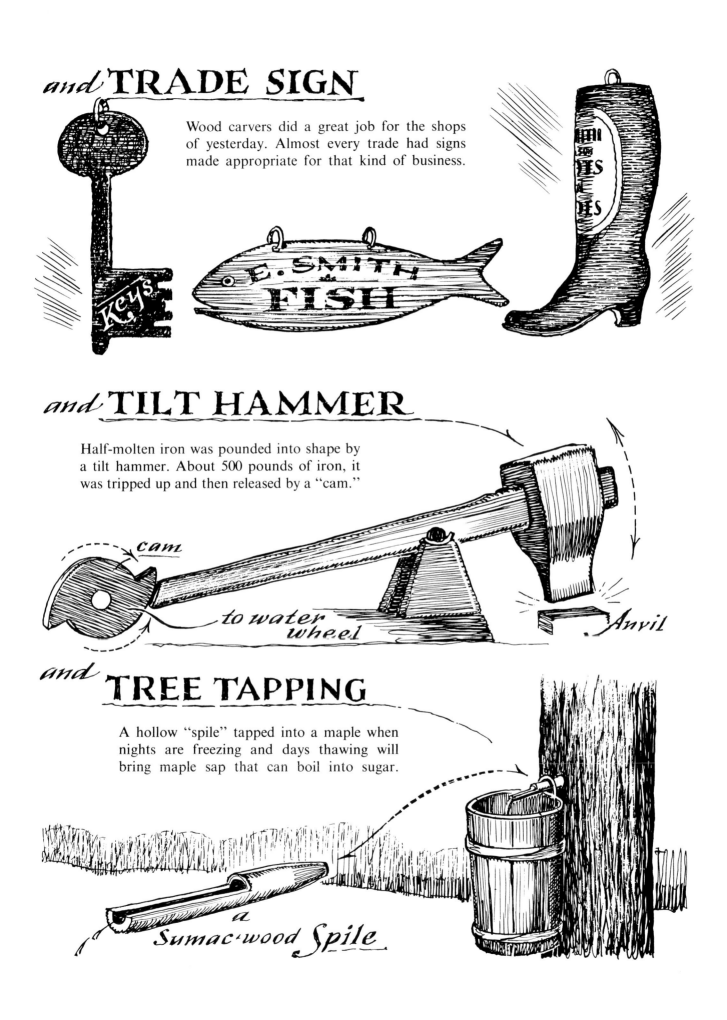

and TRADE SIGN

Wood carvers did a great job for the shops of yesterday. Almost every trade had signs made appropriate for that kind of business.

Keys

E. SMITH FISH

and TILT HAMMER

Half-molten iron was pounded into shape by a tilt hammer. About 500 pounds of iron, it was tripped up and then released by a "cam."

cam

to water wheel

Anvil

and TREE TAPPING

A hollow "spile" tapped into a maple when nights are freezing and days thawing will bring maple sap that can boil into sugar.

a Sumac-wood Spile

U is for UP·AND·DOWN SAW

This was how America's first sawmills worked.

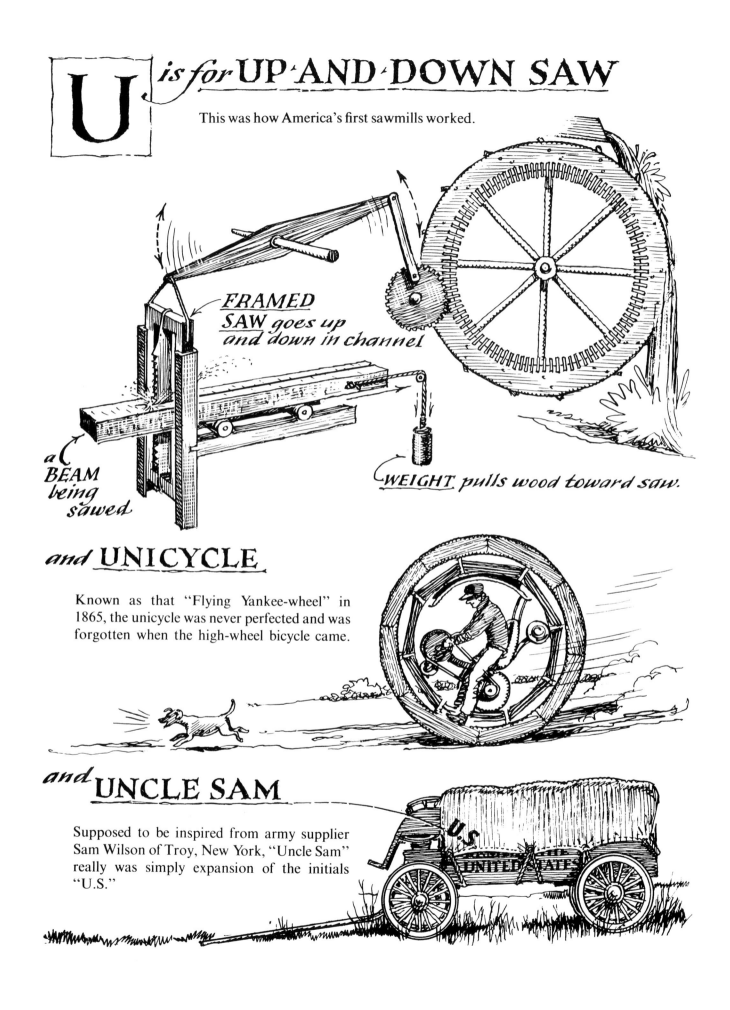

FRAMED SAW goes up and down in channel

a BEAM being sawed

WEIGHT pulls wood toward saw.

and UNICYCLE

Known as that "Flying Yankee-wheel" in 1865, the unicycle was never perfected and was forgotten when the high-wheel bicycle came.

and UNCLE SAM

Supposed to be inspired from army supplier Sam Wilson of Troy, New York, "Uncle Sam" really was simply expansion of the initials "U.S."

V is for VELOCIPEDE

Velocipedes came before bicycles. First the "fast-walker" with no pedals, then the front-wheel pedal, then a high metal back-wheeler.

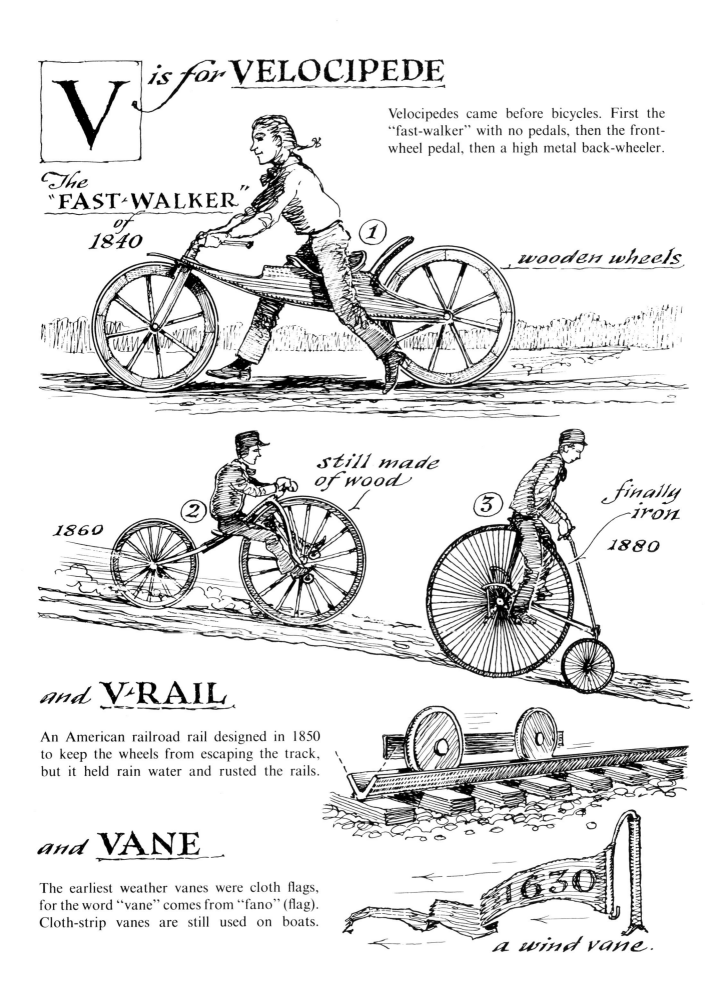

The "FAST-WALKER" of 1840

① wooden wheels

1860 ② still made of wood

③ finally iron 1880

and V-RAIL

An American railroad rail designed in 1850 to keep the wheels from escaping the track, but it held rain water and rusted the rails.

and VANE

The earliest weather vanes were cloth flags, for the word "vane" comes from "fano" (flag). Cloth-strip vanes are still used on boats.

1630

a wind vane.

W is for WATER-WHEEL

First American water mill was in Maine, 1620. For over two centuries our factories were run by three types of these wooden wheels.

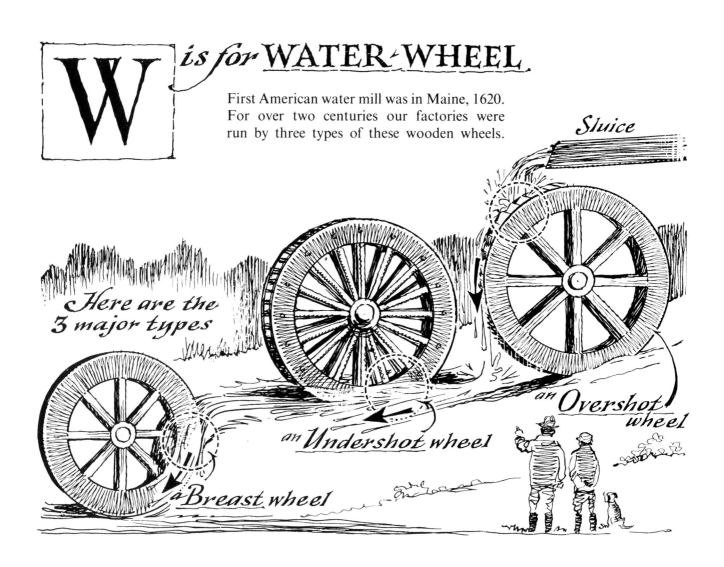

Sluice

Here are the 3 major types

an Undershot wheel

an Overshot wheel

a Breast wheel

and WEATHERVANE

Weather ruled the early American's day, and as observing wind is the best way to predict it, weathervanes were important.

1673

and WINDMILL

First windmill in America was built in 1621 in Virginia. By 1721 there were nearly a thousand.

a small portable mill.

and WITCH-HAZEL

As hazel blooms in fall and smells "wet" it was thought mystic and chosen as the wood for "divining rods" (to find water).

a Divining rod

Hold here --- and rod pulls to water.

and WHIRLING-GIG

Our word "whirligig" comes from this old farm-game device made from a pole upon a tree stump that revolves on a center pin.

a Summer Carousel or a Winter Snap-the-whip.

X is for X-BRACE

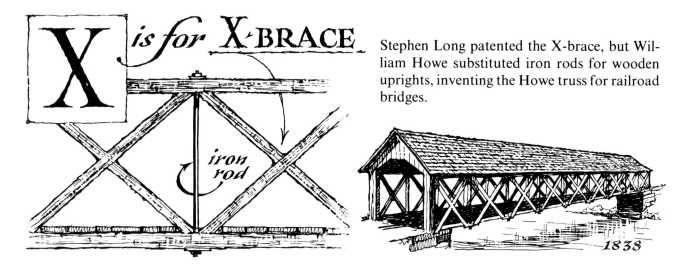

Stephen Long patented the X-brace, but William Howe substituted iron rods for wooden uprights, inventing the Howe truss for railroad bridges.

iron rod

1838

In the church, X stood for Christ (hence Xmas for Christmas) but so few words begin with X that most early American dictionaries left it out completely (Webster's, 1807, and Perry's, 1813). Listing X in alphabet books was always difficult, and some invented words as in: "Xhort with one another daily" or "X stands for Xplorer."

Y is for YANKEE *(of uncertain origin)*

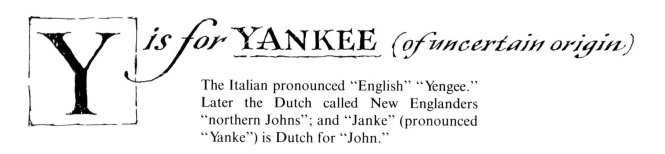

The Italian pronounced "English" "Yengee." Later the Dutch called New Englanders "northern Johns"; and "Janke" (pronounced "Yanke") is Dutch for "John."

and YOKE

Fashioned after ox yokes, early American burden carriers were made of tulipwood and used for the carrying of buckets around the old-time farmyard.

1830

Hickory hooks

Z is for Z-BRIDGE

As the side sketch shows, the early Z-bridge was made for economy, when the road reached a river at an angle instead of straight across.

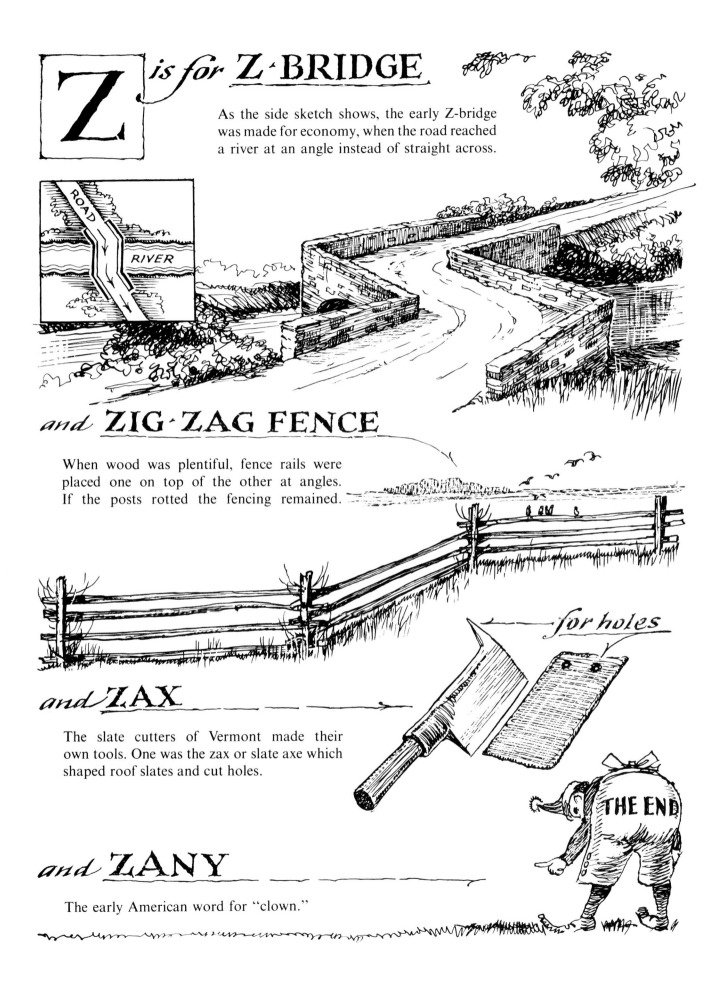

and ZIG·ZAG FENCE

When wood was plentiful, fence rails were placed one on top of the other at angles. If the posts rotted the fencing remained.

and ZAX

for holes

The slate cutters of Vermont made their own tools. One was the zax or slate axe which shaped roof slates and cut holes.

THE END

and ZANY

The early American word for "clown."

The Alphabet and Early America

As if in homage to the language and its letters that were so much a part of their new national heritage, the early American people seemed to have a peculiar reverence for their alphabet. When they couldn't think of any other decoration for a quilt or a piece of furniture or some example of sewing, they just put a fancy alphabet on it. A farmer might find difficulty in buying store-bought toys, yet he could always saw out blocks of wood and put letters on them. And he did.

There were samplers and rulers and macaroni and quilts and cakes and diaries and slates and an unending number of things with the alphabet on them. Luckily for historians there isn't a better way to express one's individuality or the times in which one lives than by handwriting or hand lettering. Anyone trained in calligraphy (the study of writing and lettering) can tell so much about the people and the history of early America. How lucky are we that the pioneers left so many calligraphic records behind!

"a GINGERBREAD HORN

for Christmas morn —
to greet the day
when Christ was born".

Old rhyme

In the early days there were no schoolbooks. An alphabet or other reading material had to be written out and then passed around the classroom. So a little wooden paddle was invented, made so that a paper could be written upon and then tacked to it. The handle kept it from being soiled by sometimes not-too-clean little hands. And to better preserve the paper, a transparent window of cow horn was put over it. And, the whole thing got to be called a "horn book."

Horn books were so much a part of the early American child's life that food was often baked "horn book shape" for children. At Christmas there was a gingerbread horn that had a special meaning. Eaten by the child during the Christmas holidays, so the legend went, "knowledge is thereby devoured by ye childe and a glad yeare with great wealth of learning becomes in store."

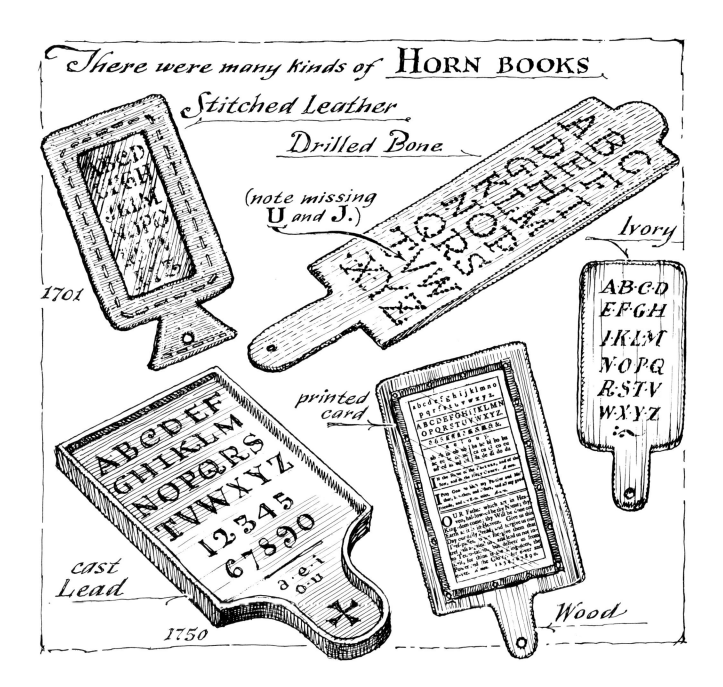

There were many kinds of HORN BOOKS

Stitched Leather

Drilled Bone

(note missing U and J.)

Ivory

1701

ABCD EFGH JKLM NOPQ RSTV WXYZ

printed card

cast Lead

ABCDEF GHIJKLM NOPQRS TVWXYZ 12345 67890

1750

Wood

On some of the horn books above you may notice that the U and the J are missing from the alphabet. Till as late as 1818, English alphabets often observed the Latin "V for U" rule while I and J were interchangeable.

One reason why horn books are so scarce is that the game of "battledore and shuttlecock" (where a feathered cork is hit back and forth by two wooden paddles) became popular just as horn books went out of style. So children made battledores (paddles) out of their horn books which soon became broken or lost.

People used to derive the greatest delight from their own making of a simple letter. They tried to put their own personality in each initial just as one does automatically with his handwriting. This explains why an early American craftsman who has made an object of rare and traditional beauty might still sign his initials in the manner of a small child, all distorted and strangely spaced. Behold, it was intentional! He had probably made those letters so, from the first day he learned to write.

Again, you may often see a beautifully carved old gravestone using classic lettering that bespeaks a knowledge of fine art and lettering; yet when one of the words came to the end of the line, there obviously wasn't enough room! So a caret was added and the remaining letter or letters were added in tiny form, carved into the marble! It doesn't make sense to us now, yet in their time it was forgivable as the essence of pure art; perhaps like some of the abstract art that we don't even understand now.

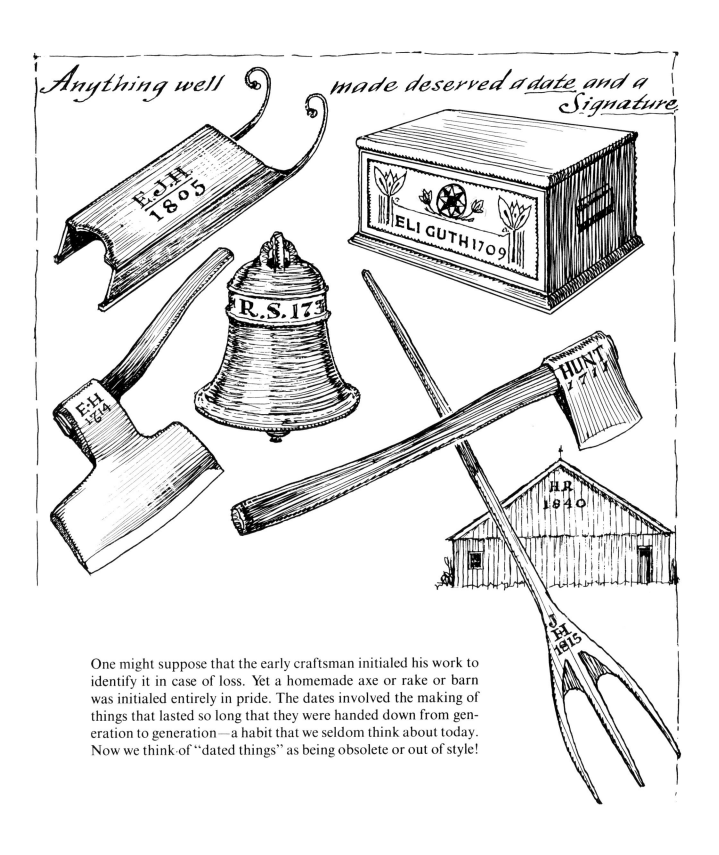

Anything well made deserved a date and a Signature

One might suppose that the early craftsman initialed his work to identify it in case of loss. Yet a homemade axe or rake or barn was initialed entirely in pride. The dates involved the making of things that lasted so long that they were handed down from generation to generation—a habit that we seldom think about today. Now we think of "dated things" as being obsolete or out of style!

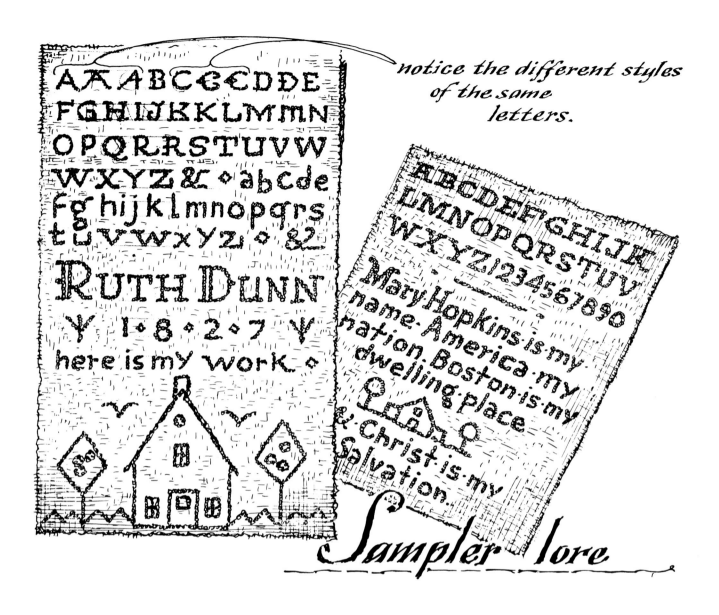

notice the different styles
of the same
letters.

A Ä A B C C Ð Ð E
F G H I J K K L M M N
O P Q R R S T U V W
W X Y Z & ◦ a b c d e
f g h i j k l m n o p q r s
t u v w x y z ◦ &
RUTH DUNN
Y 1·8·2·7 Y
here is my work ◦

A B C D E F G H I J K
L M N O P Q R S T U V
W X Y Z 1 2 3 4 5 6 7 8 9 0
Mary Hopkins is my
name. America my
nation. Boston is my
dwelling place
& Christ is my
Salvation.

Sampler lore

Samplers were sewing practice for those who hoped later to sew names upon household linens; that is why they usually began with the alphabet itself. Not reserved for children, old people often made samplers too. Catherine, the wife of Charles II, sewed:

21st of Maye
Was our Wedding Daye.

Poor rhyming though it is, here was a favorite:

This work is mine, My friends may have,
When I am Dead and laid in Grave.

So you see how samplers, like almost everything else that was handmade by the early people, were designed for keeping and for the nearly lost art of handing down to future generations.

Alas, we have everything done or made for us in this modern age, and we are deprived of the privilege and honor of putting our initials on things except for the ugly reason of keeping them from being stolen. Not so long ago when people made their own tools or furniture or houses, one of the greatest satisfactions was to put that finishing touch upon it, the date and the initials of the maker!

Satisfied, and with the hope that this simple book might give the reader something good to think about, may I then finish my creation just as the early American did, with my identifying mark?

E.S.
1963